For many years few knew who Prince Michael of Kent was. A cousin of the Queen, he is quite junior in the Royal ranks.

All this changed when he married the woman who was to say, 'I am many things but I am not boring.' Marie-Christine von Reibnitz entered Prince Michael's life while still married to her first husband and, several years later, she stormed into the headlines with a panache never before shown by British Royalty. As time went by, events were to prove so extraordinary that the couple would repeatedly find themselves in the midst of controversy. But no matter what scandal or obstacle may threaten the marriage, the Prince and his Princess will overcome it, for they are devoted to experiencing all life's adventures together.

TROUBLED CHILDHOODS

ALTHOUGH THEY GREW UP ON OPPOSITE SIDES OF THE WORLD, PRINCE MICHAEL OF KENT AND MARIE-CHRISTINE VON REIBNITZ SHARED SIGNIFICANT EARLY EXPERIENCES: BOTH WERE RAISED ON MODEST MEANS AND WITHOUT FATHERS

♔ Poor little not-so-rich boy Prince Michael below was orphaned before his first birthday. His widowed mother was not supported by the Civil List and so had to bring up her three young children as frugally as royally possible on her relatively modest income

Hulton Picture Company

PRINCE MICHAEL WAS THE THIRD CHILD of George, Duke of Kent, the youngest surviving son of George V. The Duke of Kent was the best-looking of the Windsor boys, taller and more manly than his two elder brothers David and Bertie, and more intellectual, artistic and musical than all of George V's children put together. He was very charming and his mother's favourite. But George was the least stable of the family, with a temperament unsuited to the royal tradition of a career in the services. He was rebellious, openly sexually adventurous, dabbled in drugs and drank more than was good for him.

It was a relief to everyone when he married Princess Marina, the beautiful, stylish Greek Princess, who shared his intellectual and artistic inclinations. They were very well matched.

Their first child was Prince Edward, now Duke of Kent, who was born in 1935. Princess Alexandra followed on Christmas Day of the next year – 1936 – during which George V had died and Edward VIII abdicated. Prince Michael came years after. He was born on 4 July 1942. Queen Mary, visiting their country home, Coppins, on 13 August, noted, 'The baby is sweet ... Georgie looked so happy with his lovely wife and dear baby ...'

A family in despair

Less than two weeks later this family idyll was shattered. The Duke of Kent was killed in an air-crash. Prince Michael was only seven weeks old at the time.

For Marina, who was 35 at the time, her husband's death marked the moment when she finally grew up. Until that time she had lived happily in George's shadow. He had not only looked after the finances, he had run the house-hold: decorating their residences to his own taste and making the domestic arrangements.

Under Queen Mary's guidance and protection, Marina pulled herself together. Ten weeks after George's death she made her first official appearance. Around the same time she began to take charge of her affairs, and what she found came as a shock.

While George was alive they had received a large sum from the Civil List for carrying out their Royal duties. This ceased on his death: no provision had been made for Royal widows. George, blithely unaware, of course, that he would die so young and leave Marina in such a difficult situation, had willed his money to his children, tied up in trust funds until they came of age so that there was nothing for Marina. The only money she was entitled to was a small widow's pension from the RAF, but she felt that taking this would be undignified.

A modest life style

To make ends meet Marina had to economize. She kept a staff of butler, footman, personal maid, housemaid, cook, assistant cook, two daily women and two part-time gardeners. Their wages were lower than average, but they were devoted to her and proud to be in her service.

This, by Royal standards at the time, was a modest retinue, and to finance it Marina started to sell off some of the art treasures her husband

Dorothy Wilding Camera Press

Thoroughly modern parents left Prince George and Princess Marina were the darlings of Society. A Royal tearaway, George was generally regarded as a gay young man and Marina, a Royal Princess of Greece, was renowned for her sense of style. Together, they brought a cosmopolitan elegance to the British Royal Family

Born on the fourth of July, Prince Michael was christened, a month later, Michael George Charles Franklin – the last name in honour of President Roosevelt of the USA, a family friend, who was, however, unable to be present at the christening at Windsor below

Popperfoto

MOTHER'S LITTLE HELPER

Princess Alexandra, Prince Michael's elder sister, spent a happy and boisterous childhood – first, during the war, under the wing of her grandmother, Queen Mary, and later at Coppins, the family home. In the relaxed and informal atmosphere fostered by Princess Marina, mother and daughter *right* enjoyed a closeness rare among Royals then. At 12, she went to Heathfield, the first Royal princess to attend school. Alexandra was recruited early into the rounds of Royal duties. But under the expert tutelage of her mother, she soon acquired poise and sophistication and won over the public with her sincere warmth and spontaneity

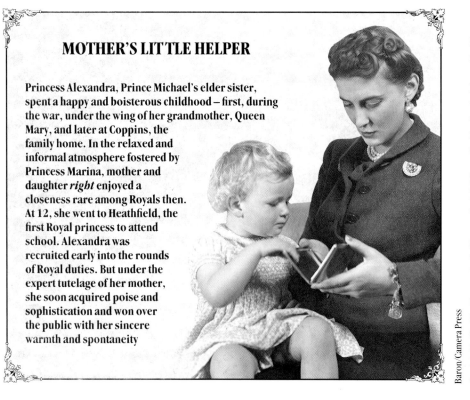

Baron/Camera Press

Both Queen Mary and George VI helped her out by making her a small allowance each from their own private money.

This, then, was the atmosphere in which Prince Michael grew up: on the outer fringes of the Royal Family in moderately straitened circumstances, with a mother who did her best to make ends meet while keeping up the appearance of Royal grandeur and ease.

He spent much of his first three years with his brother and sister at Badminton, being looked after by Queen Mary. The war was still on and it was considered the safest place to be.

The war over, they continued to live frugally. They kept their clothes, handing them down until they wore out, holidayed simply by the sea, rode on second-hand bicycles.

Prince Michael was a happy little boy, but the fact that his siblings were so much older made him something of a loner. Princess Alexandra was the first Royal girl to be sent to school, and the Duke of Kent was at Eton. Michael spent a lot of time alone with his governess, Miss Catherine Peebles.

The unknown Prince

Prince Michael followed his brother to Eton and then to Sandhurst, after which he was gazetted to the 11th Hussars. In 1968, he was appointed to serve at the Ministry of Defence as an intelligence officer.

Prince Michael had developed into a remarkable man. This almost unknown Prince

had collected. She also sold the lease on their London home in Belgrave Square with all its contents and rented out some of the land surrounding Coppins, their country home. She continued to dress superbly by making arrangements with dress designers to borrow clothes that she would return after wearing them once to a public function.

'Georgie looked so happy with his lovely wife and dear baby'

QUEEN MARY

♛ *The baby of the family, Prince Michael was loved and spoiled by his elder brother, Prince Edward, and sister, Princess Alexandra right. The Kent children were brought up not to feel special in any way; they were taught the value of money and even grew their own vegetables*

Hulton Picture Company

was now strikingly handsome, very like his father in looks. He had become increasingly independent though somewhat shy, with a passion for dangerous sports. Only the luck of the devil had stopped him being seriously hurt as he competed at international level in bobsleigh, powerboat and motor races, winning many trophies.

He was highly respected at work too: he could speak Russian – he was the first member of the Royal Family to do so – and was fluent in French and German.

At this time the general public hardly knew of his existence, upstaged as he was by his sister, Princess Alexandra, and by the fact of his brother's popular marriage to Katharine Worsley, who had become an exemplary Duchess of Kent. The few times Prince Michael was seen in public were with his mother on his arm, as he accompanied her to the opera and the theatre. The press barely mentioned him, certainly rarely speculated on his marriage prospects, and he was able to pursue his romantic course without interference.

A Baroness is born

The woman who was to become his wife was born a Baroness on 15 January 1945 on her mother's estate at Tachau in Czechoslovakia, and was given the imposing name of Marie-Christine Anne Agnes Hedwig Ida von Reibnitz. Her family background was impeccably aristocratic, with many European Royal connections. Her Hungarian mother, Countess Marianne Szapary, the daughter of Princess Hedwig, was a beautiful, intelligent and athletic woman, who was among the competitors in the Hungarian ski team at the Olympics in 1936. From the time she first heard about Hitler she was a virulent anti-Nazi and took part in anti-German, anti-Nazi demonstrations.

In 1941, when she was 30, she met her husband-to-be, the 47-year-old Czechoslovakian, Baron Gunther von Reibnitz. He had joined the Nazi party in 1930 – along with many other Catholic aristocrats – because Hitler was seen as their protector against the Communist Russians bent on overthrowing the aristocracy. But by 1941 the Baron was thoroughly disillusioned by the Nazis; he had made no public disavowal of Nazism but was only an honorary member of the SS-Gestapo, with no military duties. 'I wouldn't even have gone on talking to him if he had still thought Hitler's regime was a good thing,' his wife has said.

By 1944 the Baron was totally disenchanted with the Nazi party. His wife was under suspicion because she had publicly refused to give the Heil Hitler salute and had been caught listening to the BBC – an act amounting to treachery. She was called to

appear before the Gestapo to account for her behaviour. The Baron stood by her, after which he was expelled from the SS, thrown out of the Nazi party and sent to Russia to fight. He was soon captured and taken as a prisoner of war.

The Countess continued her anti-Nazi activities. She had a small son and was pregnant with her second child, but she refused to keep a low profile. She was arrested while taking part in an anti-Nazi demonstration and was tried once again. Although she was eight months pregnant she was made to stand throughout the two-week trial, at the end of which she was sent to a concentration camp. By some quirk of compassion she was released in time to give birth to Marie-Christine.

👑 *Home sweet home for the young Michael was Coppins in Buckinghamshire above. Left to his parents by Princess Victoria, George V's sister, its cosy, relaxed atmosphere matched the unstuffy image of the Kents*

👑 *Three men in a boat below: Prince Michael centre with his Gloucester cousins the Princes William left and Richard right at Barnwell Manor, where Michael first met Marie-Christine in 1972. Her first husband, Tom Troubridge, had been at Eton with Prince William*

5

By now the tide was turning in the war, and the Russians were advancing across Europe. Caught between two evils, the family had to flee their castle. Marie-Christine was only a few months old.

Escape to safety

With the help of her brother, the children's governess and her maid, the Countess Marianne loaded as many possessions as she could on to a cart drawn by two horses and made her way through the forests of her estate into the safety of Bavaria. The things in the cart were covered with hay and the baby Marie-Christine was perched on top. Once the children were safe, the Countess and her brother returned to salvage what they could from the castle before it was taken by the Russians, and their final haul included a fortune in diamonds.

The Countess still had a house in Kitzbühel, where they set up home. She was grief-stricken, having heard that her husband had died in a Russian prisoner-of-war camp. In fact, while the camp guards celebrated Russian victories by drinking themselves insensible, the Baron had escaped and soon made his way home to his family.

At the end of 1947 the Baron was tried by a Bavarian de-Nazification court. Their findings were that, although he had at one time been a Nazi follower, he had never been a supporter, and had been against the regime. The subject was closed and the terrible fact that he had once been a Nazi was never spoken about in the family. Marie-Christine was brought up knowing about her parents' opposition to Nazism and nothing else – an omission she was to come to regret in later life.

A MYSTERIOUS TRAGEDY

The Duke of Kent kissed his wife goodbye on 23 August 1942, expecting to return shortly. Two days later he was among the 15 people who boarded a flying boat captained by a very capable pilot and with an experienced crew of nine. Although the weather was poor, the Cromarty Firth was fairly clear and conditions were expected to improve by the time they reached open sea.

Although the plane was supposed to follow the Scottish coastline, for some unknown reason it headed inland and, near the village of Berriedale, the plane cleared a 900-foot summit known as Eagles Rock. It did not clear the next rise. As the plane crashed into the hillside, the sound of two explosions reverberated through the hills.

The next morning, the wreckage was found and George's body identified. An investigation into the cause of the crash was carried out, but the final decision, which put the blame on the captain, was controversial. And despite many subsequent theories that have been formulated over the years, the Duke of Kent's fatal flight is still shrouded in mystery

Popperfoto

👑 Below *Under cover at Eton. Prince Michael is sheltered by Prince William while chatting to the Gloucesters* right *and Michael's sister, Alexandra,* left. *Michael had gone up the year before, at the age of 13*

Countess Marianne's problems were not over with the ending of the war. The Baron finally confessed to her that when they had married he had assumed he would be killed in the war and had wanted to snatch a few months of happiness.

A bigamous marriage

The unfortunate truth was that he was already married with a teenage daughter. Their bigamous marriage was now, of course, invalid. As a Catholic the Countess Marianne knew that as she had married him in good faith the children were legitimate in the eyes of the Church, but she could no longer live with him. The Baron left her and his children and moved to Africa.

Marie-Christine's mother felt there was nothing left for her in Europe. With her son and five-year-old daughter, she emigrated to Australia. The family settled in Sydney and after a while Countess Marianne remarried.

Despite the titles and a few remaining heirlooms in the form of jewels and paintings, Marie-Christine now lived the life of an ordinary Australian schoolgirl.

Their house was modest, they had no servants, and they lived more frugally than her new friends at the smart girls' school which she eventually attended as a weekly boarder. She was a scholarship girl: her mother couldn't

Hulton Picture Company

afford to pay the fees.

It is not hard to imagine the impact that this fractured past had on the young Marie-Christine. Her mother's stories were of wealth, grandeur and unimaginable sufferings. Yet to the girls she went around with, her family were merely odd, funny foreigners, rather poor, and the fact that they had titles cut no ice in egalitarian Australia.

What Marie-Christine's mother wanted for her daughter more than anything was a good education. Having experienced the fragility of good fortune in the form of money and high birth, she felt that her daughter's future was dependent only on her brain. She had been very academic herself, and her motto was 'no child of mine ever fails an exam'; a friend described her as 'a total blue-stocking, uninterested in glamour or social standing'.

Clever and hardworking

Marie-Christine did not let her mother down. She worked hard at school and excelled in sport as well: she was good at tennis, swimming and riding. She went to evening classes to learn to sew so that she could supplement her limited budget by making her own clothes.

She was still only 15 in December 1960 when she passed out of school with honours, the youngest girl ever to do so in New South Wales. She was too young to go to university and her mother agreed that she could go to stay with her father in Mozambique instead. The last time she had seen him was when she was less than five years old.

When she saw her 67-year-old father she was stunned: 'He seemed old enough to be my grandfather,' she later said. But she soon recovered from the shock and enjoyed her time in Africa with him. It couldn't have been more different from the modest Sydney suburban life she had known in recent years.

Two years later Marie-Christine was back in Sydney. By now she knew that what she wanted to do was return to her roots in Europe. To make the necessary money she set up a business designing clothes and soon had the capital she needed.

Her European tour started in Trieste; from there she went to Venice and then to Vienna, where she stayed a year. She studied art history in Florence, Vienna and Pisa, and it was during this period that she decided she wanted to make her career as an interior designer.

The move to London

In 1965 Marie-Christine came to Britain. A friend of her mother lent her a small flat in Eaton Square and she found work as an apprentice interior designer doing the menial jobs of stripping wallpaper, simple carpentry, and

PA/Topham

whatever else needed to be done. After a while she took a job as a secretary in an advertising agency. This, she decided, was essential to give her experience of office administration – she was not interested in the secretarial aspect. 'She was poised, self-confident and charming. She was very good at meeting people, organizing and talking to clients over the telephone,' said her boss. 'But she was inclined to talk to clients as though she was an executive, she was mis-cast as a secretary.'

Not only was she mis-cast, Marie-Christine was more interested in her social life outside office hours, and was constantly late. Finally, and not surprisingly, it was politely put to her that she might be happier employed somewhere more flexible.

By then Marie-Christine had learned what she needed to know. She set up her own interior design business called Szapary Designs. She was an instant success and still in her early 20s. She was rich, admired, sought after. The next step was marriage.

♕ *Eyes right at Sandhurst* above. *After Eton, Michael wanted to join the Navy, but failed the rigorous eye test, and so joined the Hussars as a cadet at the Royal Military Academy in 1961. He passed out the next year, a professional soldier but still retaining the fresh-faced charm that had earned him the nickname 'Cherub' there*

♕ *Marie-Christine had an exciting early life, though later she was brought up a suburban schoolgirl in Australia. Unfortunately, after the adverse – and largely malicious – press attention she received in 1985, information about Her Royal Highness's early life was curtailed, resulting in a universal shortage of pictorial material concerning her before her Royal marriage*

♛ Princess Michael enjoys wearing items from her outstanding jewellery collection at public functions and when entertaining. She is shown *left* at Queen Charlotte's Hospital Anniversary Ball on 21 July 1989, wearing one of her splendid diamond tiaras, a pair of diamond hoop earrings with diamond centres hanging from small collet diamonds – inherited from Princess Marina – and a seven-stranded necklace of pearls with elaborate clasps

♛ Prince and Princess Michael are photographed at Kensington Palace *below* in September 1981, before setting off on their flight to Belize to represent the Queen at the independence celebrations. The Princess is wearing the diamond fringe tiara Princess Marina received as a wedding present, the hoop earrings worn in the photo *left* but with sapphire centres instead of diamond ones, and twin crescent clips of diamonds and sapphires (one is hidden by her right sleeve). The Prince wears tropical dress uniform of the Royal Hussars

Rex

David Bailey/Camera Press

A MAGNIFICENT COLLECTION

Princess Michael has inherited many fabulous pieces of jewellery. Most came from her mother-in-law, Princess Marina of Greece, others from the collection once owned by Princess Hedwig Windisch-Graetz, her grandmother. Their total value has been estimated at around two million pounds. Although retired from active service after 20 years, Prince Michael wears Royal Hussars uniform when representing the Queen

Anthony Crickmay/Camera Press

♔ *Above* Prince Michael wears Number One Dress Uniform of the Prince of Wales's Own Regiment of the Royal Hussars, in which he held the rank of Major. The photograph, taken in 1980, shows the Prince without the beard he was soon to grow

♔ In the photograph *right*, taken in July 1983, Princess Michael is wearing the diamond and pearl festoon tiara she inherited from Princess Marina, along with her sapphire and diamond earrings and twin crescent clips, and a multi-stranded pearl necklace with Princess Marina's brooch of natural pearls surrounding a large black pearl worn as a clasp

Norman Parkinson/Camera Press

A CHANCE MEETING

WHEN THEY MET AT A BARBECUE, BOTH MARIE-CHRISTINE AND PRINCE MICHAEL WERE PURSUING THEIR OWN SUCCESSFUL AND SEPARATE LIVES. NEITHER REALIZED WHERE THEIR NEW-FOUND FRIENDSHIP WOULD LEAD

T HE MARIE-CHRISTINE WHO WAS NOW impressing herself on the London scene was a stunning young woman. Her extraordinary looks meant that she was never ignored. 'I am very keen on femininity, even though I am six foot and have large bones,' she has said of herself and, with her slim figure, long hair and huge, blue eyes, her femininity has never been in doubt.

Some men must have found her formidable. 'I don't think I'm really afraid of anything,' she has said, and this was patently true even then. By any standards she had made a phenomenal success of her life by her early 20s, becoming rich in under two years without the benefit of a backer. The money she made was hers alone, and it was made in a climate more hostile

♛ *Like other members of the Royal Family, Prince Michael enjoys dangerous sports. He is seen with his car below before the start of the 1970 World Cup Rally at Wembley. Cars, whether for rally driving or general use, are one of Prince Michael's special interests – something he inherited from his father*

to the lone entrepreneur than it would be two decades later.

Marie-Christine met Tom Troubridge at a wild-boar hunt on the German estate of one of her relatives in 1969. Troubridge was a good friend of Prince William of Gloucester and, through his brother, a flag officer on the Royal yacht *Britannia*, knew other members of the Royal Family. Troubridge was a banker, part of the British branch of the Kleinwort merchant banking business. Here was a man who was not deterred by Marie-Christine's phenomenal success; indeed, he positively admired it.

Troubridge was 30 when they met, and Marie-Christine was 24. The attraction between them was very strong. They had a lot in common. Both were highly successful in their

♛ *Prince Michael and his sister, Princess Alexandra, give a standing ovation to the winner at Wimbledon above right. This was one of the few public appearances made by the young Prince, who coveted his privacy and tried to avoid the press's prying eye whenever possible*

♛ *The 25-year-old Prince arrives at Whitehall right to begin his new job with Defence Intelligence. Here he was able to put his command of the Russian language into practice by serving as a liaison officer for military attachés*

Hulton Picture Company

Topham

own right, were attractive, outgoing and popular. Troubridge was universally well liked and charming. Marie-Christine was impressed by the fact that he was well connected and he appreciated her aristocratic origins.

The couple were officially engaged on 25 May 1971. The wedding was four months later, on 15 September. A small problem was presented by the fact that Marie-Christine was a devout Catholic and Troubridge had been brought up as an Anglican. They solved this by choosing a Catholic-Anglican ceremony in the Anglican Chelsea Old Church.

An incompatible couple

Among Troubridge's friends there were those who seemed surprised that the committed bachelor had finally been caught. Others romantically put it down to the fact that the couple were so well suited. But cracks in the relationship were apparent even at the wedding itself. As the guests hung around chatting and waiting for the newlyweds to emerge from the vestry after the ceremony was over, they soon had to talk loudly to cover the sound of the 'happy couple' arguing bitterly.

The marriage was doomed from this early stage. In common with many other young couples who marry out of mutual attraction, they had neglected to find out what the other expected from the married state. Marie-Christine was looking for the very things her childhood lacked: stability, overt status, and the security of a happy married life. She had worked

'I don't think I'm really afraid of anything'

MARIE-CHRISTINE

Topham

THE 'FOURTH MAN'

By the time Prince Michael joined Intelligence as a liaison officer in 1968, the foundations of British Intelligence had been badly shaken. 1950s revelations of a Russian espionage ring involving Guy Burgess and Donald MacLean were again brought to the surface when, in 1963, Kim Philby was labelled as the 'third man'. The following year, further investigations had uncovered Anthony Blunt *left*, art adviser to the Queen, as the 'fourth'. Under interrogation, Blunt admitted to being a long-term agent for the Soviet Union. However, this news was kept top secret for a further 15 years and Blunt was granted immunity from prosecution.

While it is highly probable that the Queen was one of the few who came to know of Blunt's espionage, she did not strip him of his knighthood until his public disclosure in 1979

Hulton Picture Company

♛ *Marie-Christine and Prince Michael first met at the stately Barnwell Manor below. When the Duke and Duchess of Gloucester learned of the couple's affair years later they were less than happy about it. They had remained good friends with Troubridge, and couldn't help feeling guilty that the couple had met at their house*

♛ *Prince Michael inspects the engine of his car right during the Avon Motor Tour of Britain in 1973. The Prince, a motoring fanatic, started his collection of vehicles at a young age. This fascination with cars would soon lead him into the role of President of the Royal Automobile Club*

towards this end throughout her young life, and was now planning to give up work and enter a career as a wife and mother. Troubridge clearly thought very differently.

Shortly after her marriage Marie-Christine began an intensive art course at the Victoria and Albert Museum. Throughout this period friends were perplexed as to why she continued to accept commissions as a decorator.

The reason was that Troubridge was continuing to behave very much as he did as a bachelor. He had married a professional young woman and clearly didn't see why she should suddenly end her immensely successful career from which she had seemed to derive so much satisfaction and fulfilment.

But a more fundamental problem in the marriage soon emerged. The one argument Marie Christine could legitimately advance in favour of giving up work was that she would have to do so when they started a family. The answer was that Troubridge did not want children. To Marie-Christine, who very much did want them, this was a most unexpected blow. It had not occurred to either of them to establish how they felt on this point before they married.

With such fundamental disagreement, it was inevitable that within a year the marriage had become very shaky, though both were putting a brave face on it. They continued to lead a frenetic social life, hardly ever spending time alone together. On the weekends they went to stay with Troubridge's mother or at house parties with their wealthy friends. It was at one of these, at the home of the Duke and Duchess of Gloucester in 1972, that Marie-Christine met Prince Michael of Kent.

A memorable impact

The meeting had no immediate romantic repercussions. Marie-Christine was still hoping that the problems she had with her husband could be attributed to the normal ups and downs of the first year of marriage. Prince Michael, anyway, had brought a girlfriend with him to the Gloucesters'. But they both made an impact on each other, which they still remembered years later.

'I was very struck by this tall Austrian lady,' Prince Michael has said, remembering when they first met. 'I was very impressed. I remember we had a long talk about the history of art sitting in a hut eating sausages.'

Marie-Christine was equally impressed. 'I just thought he was the funniest man I had ever met. We just kept laughing and talking together. But I didn't think he really "noticed" me at all. He was with such a pretty girl.'

At the very least, a friendship had started and Marie-Christine was aware of the value of this new acquaintance. He soon became a regular at the dinner parties she gave. The 'pretty girl' he had been with at the Gloucesters turned out to be an unimportant relationship, and he was often without a special girlfriend.

'He was a charming spare man I used to invite to dinner parties or when I had extremely eligible European relatives over,' Marie-Christine said years later. 'I thought, this young man is all alone, I'll produce the right girlfriend for him. I saw myself as a sort of fairy godmother, waving my magic wand.'

But before too long something happened that would decisively change Marie-Christine's relationship with her husband.

In late 1972 Tom was posted to Bahrain. It was accepted by both of them that Marie-Christine would come with him. This was the chance for them to live the life of a conventional, married couple that Marie-Christine had

previously craved. She fixed up one design commission in Bahrain, but when this was over she had nothing to do but play the wife.

The result was acutely uncomfortable for both of them. Marie-Christine, far from the life she knew, without her friends and with no work to occupy her, concentrated her attentions on Tom. She was soon made inescapably aware of the fact that 'he had no need of me'.

Return to London

When it became clear that things were getting worse between them it seemed pointless for Marie-Christine to remain in Bahrain. Before long she had made the decision to come back to London. She settled back in their home and picked up the threads of her business again.

Marie-Christine's social life picked up too, and it was inevitable that she would start to see her 'charming spare man', Prince Michael.

If there was an attraction between them, both were concerned to control it. To begin with they met strictly as friends, and indeed Prince Michael was rarely without a date.

The nature of the friendship started to change after one particular occasion when they had lunch together. Prince Michael had just finished his relationship with Patricia Rawlings, a woman with whom he had been very much in love. Marie-Christine was feeling

'I just thought he was the funniest man I had ever met'

MARIE-CHRISTINE ON MICHAEL

♛ *As a past winner of the British Bobsleigh Championship in 1972, Prince Michael was well-suited to his role as President of the British Bobsleigh Association. He announces a sponsorship boost for the British Team in 1978* below

John Shelley

Hulton Picture Company

Hulton Picture Company

fragile too. The longer she lived apart from her husband, the more convinced she was that her marriage was over. They spent the lunch commiserating with each other and talking compulsively about their own problems.

This created an intimacy – and a sympathy – between them. They started to meet more regularly. 'For a long time we cried on each other's shoulders,' Marie-Christine has said. 'I saw him for about a year simply as a friend. Now I'm very glad we had that time because friendship is something you never lose – and when you're in the rocking chair, friendship is what counts.'

Prince Michael was by this time based in London so there were many more opportunities to meet. Between 1974 and 1976 he was back at the Ministry of Defence serving as an Intelligence Officer, where his command of the Russian language made him an invaluable member of staff.

The friendship between Marie-Christine and Prince Michael slowly developed throughout 1974. Now that she was getting to know him better, Marie-Christine could allow herself to admit that she had in fact been 'immediately and forcefully' impressed by the Prince, particularly by his physical courage. 'I love bravery,'

she has said, and she has no lack of it herself. It is important for her that she can look up to the man in her life in this aspect. Prince Michael did not let her down: 'He will take on the most terrifying things, not in a daredevil way but simply refusing to be afraid.'

Love blossoms

Prince Michael became aware that he was falling in love with Marie-Christine. He knew that she went out riding every morning in Richmond Park, and after a while he started to do the same. She was pleased and somewhat bemused when they began to bump into each other in the early mornings. In fact, riding was not a great love of his, and this had only been a ploy to see her more often.

It became inevitable that their relationship should deepen. However they arranged their meetings with the utmost discretion. Their favourite mode of transport became Prince Michael's motorbike, which gave them welcome anonymity under the helmets.

At the beginning of their relationship, neither Marie-Christine nor Prince Michael realized how important they were going to be to each other. But after three years they had to acknowledge that what had started as a friend-

---

THE ROYAL MATCHMAKER

Hulton Picture Company

The match between Marie-Christine and Prince Michael was advanced and encouraged by Lord Mountbatten, who had taken an avuncular interest in Prince Michael ever since his father had died.

Mountbatten's relationship as friend and valued adviser of the Queen meant that he had been able to intercede on behalf of the younger Kents whenever he felt it necessary. For instance, he had helped smooth the way for Prince Michael's elder brother to leave the army and take a directorship.

Marie-Christine seemed to him to be an ideal wife for Prince Michael, notwithstanding the fact that she was a Catholic and already married. Mountbatten was most impressed by Marie-Christine's family tree, which gave her an impeccably aristocratic European background.

Under the Royal Marriages Act of 1772, the Queen had to give her consent before the couple could be allowed to marry. Mountbatten told them to keep their intentions secret and to leave the negotiations to him. His gentle reasoning and absolute conviction that this marriage was right was essential in helping the Queen make up her mind

☙ *Prince Michael and Marie-Christine make one of their first public appearances together right. For years they had kept their interest in each other a secret to avoid a scandal. Even after their relationship had become quite serious, very few people were aware of their intentions*

Hulton Picture Company

♛ *Prince William of Gloucester above was the cousin of Prince Michael as well as a good friend of Tom Troubridge. He was the link that made possible that first meeting between Marie-Christine and Prince Michael*

ship was now a matter of extreme seriousness.

By this time all their friends and closest relatives knew about the relationship. Even Troubridge had been told – and he accepted that his marriage had broken up well before Prince Michael had come on to the scene.

Mr Right

Marie-Christine now had no doubt that she had met the man with whom she wanted to spend her life. Besides his Royal status, his looks, his intellect and his courage, she was drawn to the fact that he was a deeply honourable man, something that she has continued to value in him through the years. 'I know that here is someone who will always do what is right. If I am in any doubt on an issue, I know his instincts will be right.'

Lord Mountbatten was one of the first members of the Royal Family to know about the relationship, and he approved of it despite the fact that Marie-Christine was married. She called him her 'good angel', and was indebted to him for the fact that he felt that they should marry despite the drawbacks. With his European connections, he had come across many members of her family throughout the years. 'Knowing my family was one of the things that decided him that my husband and I would "work",' she said years later. 'In many ways he made our marriage – without his support and help championing our cause, I doubt whether it would have happened.'

As early as 1976 Mountbatten told Marie-Christine that she 'ought to marry that young man'. She asked him why and he replied, 'Because he is madly in love with you.' But although this was what Marie-Christine wanted, she felt sure that it was impossible. She knew that Prince William of Gloucester had asked the Queen for permission to marry the woman he loved, Nicole Sieff, but had been refused on the grounds that she was a divorcee.

The inevitable decision

How much less chance did she, Marie-Christine, have? She would be divorced and a Catholic as well, a combination unlikely to endear her to the Queen. Realistically it didn't seem a possibility worth contemplating.

But whether she was to marry Prince Michael or not, Marie-Christine knew that she could no longer stay married to Troubridge. The divorce was easy to obtain on the grounds that they had been separated for more than three years. It went through smoothly and without acrimony. But for Marie-Christine, a devout Catholic, this was not good enough. In the eyes of the Church she was still married.

Marie-Christine applied for an annulment on the grounds that her husband would not give her children. This process involved lengthy interviews with Roman Catholic clergy and statements from her ex-husband, family and friends. In 1978 her application was granted. At last she was free technically and religiously. But would that be good enough for the British Royal Family?

Hulton Picture Company

'*I know that here is someone who will always do what is right*'
MARIE-CHRISTINE ON MICHAEL

♛ *Below* Princess Michael's gold silk dress is enhanced by a fabulous set of jewels comprising a necklace, earrings and brooch made of seed pearls, diamonds and aquamarines

Photographers International

Multi-stranded deep pearl choker

Gown nipped in at the waist with decoratively shaped belt

See-through Chantilly lace (very delicate bobbin lace) panels on bodice, sleeves and skirt

Flounces of Chantilly lace inserted vertically into skirt of the gown.

♛ The gown worn by Marie-Christine on the evening of her Viennese wedding *right* was designed by Bellville Sassoon of Britain. Made from cream silk crêpe de Chine, the dress has a pin-tucked bodice with a deep see-through yoke, finished at its lower edge with a deep lace trim. The skirt has a small train and is decorated with vertical lace inserts and lace trim at the hem

Lynne Robinson

A CERTAIN SENSE OF STYLE

Princess Michael is a very tall and striking woman whose self-professed 'foreign shape' has a substantial influence on her clothes. An innate understanding of how colours and cuts can be used to compliment her figure has always governed her style sense. The Princess does not allow passing fashion trends to rule her decisions, as this selection of her evening wear shows

♛ Princess Michael wears an unusual full-length evening-gown *right*. The shimmering sheath of pale pink satin has been slashed diagonally with a panel of black velvet. Black velvet also forms the crossover halter-neck bodice

Diamond and sapphire jewellery, earrings and twin clasps

Dress bodice gathered and draped around midriff and hips

Full length, sun-ray pleated skirt

John Shelley

♛ *Above* With a luxurious gown of white and ivory patterned brocade, Marie-Christine wears a five-stranded pearl choker studded with diamond clasps and pearl and diamond earrings

Lush off-the-shoulder velvet shawl neckline tied into a large bow

Bracelet-length full sleeves gathered into narrow cuffs

Glen Harvey/Camera Press

♛ This romantic white gown *above* has a full chiffon skirt and a satin bodice overlaid with lace. Adorning Marie-Christine's shoulders are dusty blue satin roses, and around her neck is a pearl choker

Full-length, bell-shaped skirt which gathers into the waist

♛ Full dresses made from luxurious fabrics, like this one of heavy velvet and lengths of striped lilac satin *left*, are favoured by the Princess

Black bandeau top worn beneath split-fronted dress bodice

Waist-hugging deep satin belt trimmed with gem-studded buckle

♛ This stylish evening-gown *left* is fashioned from heavy black satin, appliquéd all over with a red satin rose and leaf motif. The outfit is completed by long black satin gloves and jewels of pearls and diamonds

Circular jewelled brooches worn at bodice and skirt vents

John Shelley

♛ *Above* The Princess wore this multi-coloured gown to an event at the Barbican in 1989. The body-skimming dress has a dramatic slash down the back of the bodice. The skirt hugs the hips and fans out towards the hem, which has been trimmed with *diamanté*

LOVE FINDS A WAY

AS A DIVORCEE AND A CATHOLIC, MARIE-CHRISTINE WAS DOUBTFUL THAT THE QUEEN WOULD CONSENT TO THE MARRIAGE. BUT ROYAL APPROVAL DID COME AND, IN THE END, IT WAS THE CHURCH THAT PROVED ITSELF THE MOST STUBBORN

MOUNTBATTEN DID AN EXCELLENT JOB OF selling Marie-Christine's credentials to the Queen – perhaps too well. After he had finished his highly coloured, detailed description of all branches of her family tree, the Queen observed drily, 'She sounds far too grand for us.' This is a quote that Mountbatten subsequently dined out on, and which has come to be widely known because of the aptness with which it seemed to describe Marie-Christine's behaviour in the years that followed her marriage.

As the Queen was fully briefed on Marie-Christine's background by Mountbatten and others, it is very unlikely that she knew nothing about Marie-Christine's father's unhappy in-

> **'I believe that every man has a special place in his heart for one woman above all others'**
>
> PRINCE MICHAEL

⚜ *With all obstacles from the Palace removed, Prince Michael and Marie-Christine were free at last to announce their engagement and bring their secret love out into the open* **right**

⚜ *One of the tallest women to marry into the Royal Family, Marie-Christine had to step down beside her fiancé to achieve a suitably romantic effect for the official engagement photograph taken by Lord Lichfield* **left**. *So successful was this ploy that the Royal photographer repeated it three years later for the similarly romantic, if more celebrated, one of the Prince of Wales and Lady Diana Spencer*

Patrick Lichfield/Camera Press

volvement with the Nazis. From her point of view the fact would have been seen as unfortunate – but it would have been no reason to veto the marriage. After all, Prince Philip's sisters had all been married to senior German officers during the war, but Philip's allegiance to Britain was never in question. Marie-Christine could not be blamed for what her father had done during the war, even had the records not shown that he had communicated his growing anti-Nazi feelings without regard to his own or his family's safety.

Family crisis
Mountbatten did not have to press the Queen too hard before she agreed to let the marriage take place. For what Marie-Christine did not know was that a momentous event was about to occur in the Royal Family that was to change the Queen's attitude to divorce.

The previously unbelievable was happening – the Queen's sister, Princess Margaret, who had been officially separated from her husband, was soon to be divorced. This event would bring divorce the closest it had been to the throne since the Queen's uncle, the Prince of Wales, had abdicated to marry the divorcee Mrs Simpson. With such an unprecedented upheaval in the Queen's immediate family, she was unlikely to stand in the way of her more remote cousin Prince Michael's marriage. Although there still remained the 'Catholic problem', that could be dealt with as well.

By early 1978 the Queen had unofficially given her consent to the marriage. That February, Marie-Christine and Prince Michael went to see Dr Coggan, the Archbishop of Canterbury, to talk about the implications of the marriage. Together they talked through the religious and constitutional problems that would be raised. Most would be solved if Prince

Syndication International

♔ ***The father of the bride arrives for the wedding* above. *It was the first time in nearly 16 years that Baron Gunther von Reibnitz had seen Marie-Christine. After the War, he had settled in Mozambique and remarried twice. In 1985 Marie-Christine was to suffer adverse publicity because of his former membership of Hitler's SS, a fact she was quite unaware of***

Michael were to renounce his place in the succession, which he indicated that he would be glad to do, but his children's rights would be unaffected if they were brought up Anglicans.

Royal consent

Under the Royal Marriages Act it is not enough for the Queen's permission alone to be obtained. According to the system, she also has to consult the Prime Minister and call a Privy Council meeting to put the question before them. This she duly did on behalf of Prince Michael, and no objections were made.

For Prince Michael and Marie-Christine the Queen's consent and approval was a great relief – and delight. The Queen let them know that they were free to marry; the only proviso she made was that they should wait until the news of Princess Margaret's divorce had been broken in the press and the first interest had died down.

Their engagement was finally announced on 30 May 1978. The Queen let it be known at the same time that after the marriage Marie-Christine was to be called Her Royal Highness Princess Michael of Kent.

No one had paid much attention to Prince Michael before his engagement was announced, but Marie-Christine was a godsend to the press. Never before had such a glamorous bride-to-be appeared on the Royal scene (Diana, after all, was still at school). Interest was strengthened by the fact that Marie-Christine was a woman rather than a young girl, over 30 with a gloriously entangled storybook past. It soon became obvious that she had another virtue as far as the press were concerned: she was frank and outspoken, and disarmingly inclined to put her foot in it.

As Marie-Christine said later, 'We didn't realize we would be so public. My husband never had been, so we didn't think anybody would find us all that interesting. We thought we'd be able to slip in under the woodwork.'

No one who knew Marie-Christine could quite credit this comment. It had never been Marie-Christine's style to slip in unnoticed anywhere, and it is unlikely that she really hoped that no-one would find her all that interesting. But what she was unprepared for was the million and one ways she could get things wrong.

'Everyone thinks that before you marry into the family you know what you are doing and what you are getting into,' she explained. 'I have heard . . . that I must have known because the Royal Family is so *visible*. But there is no way that you know what it's going to be like.'

Marie-Christine's mistake was in believing that, despite everything, she had a fairly good idea what it would be like. 'When my husband

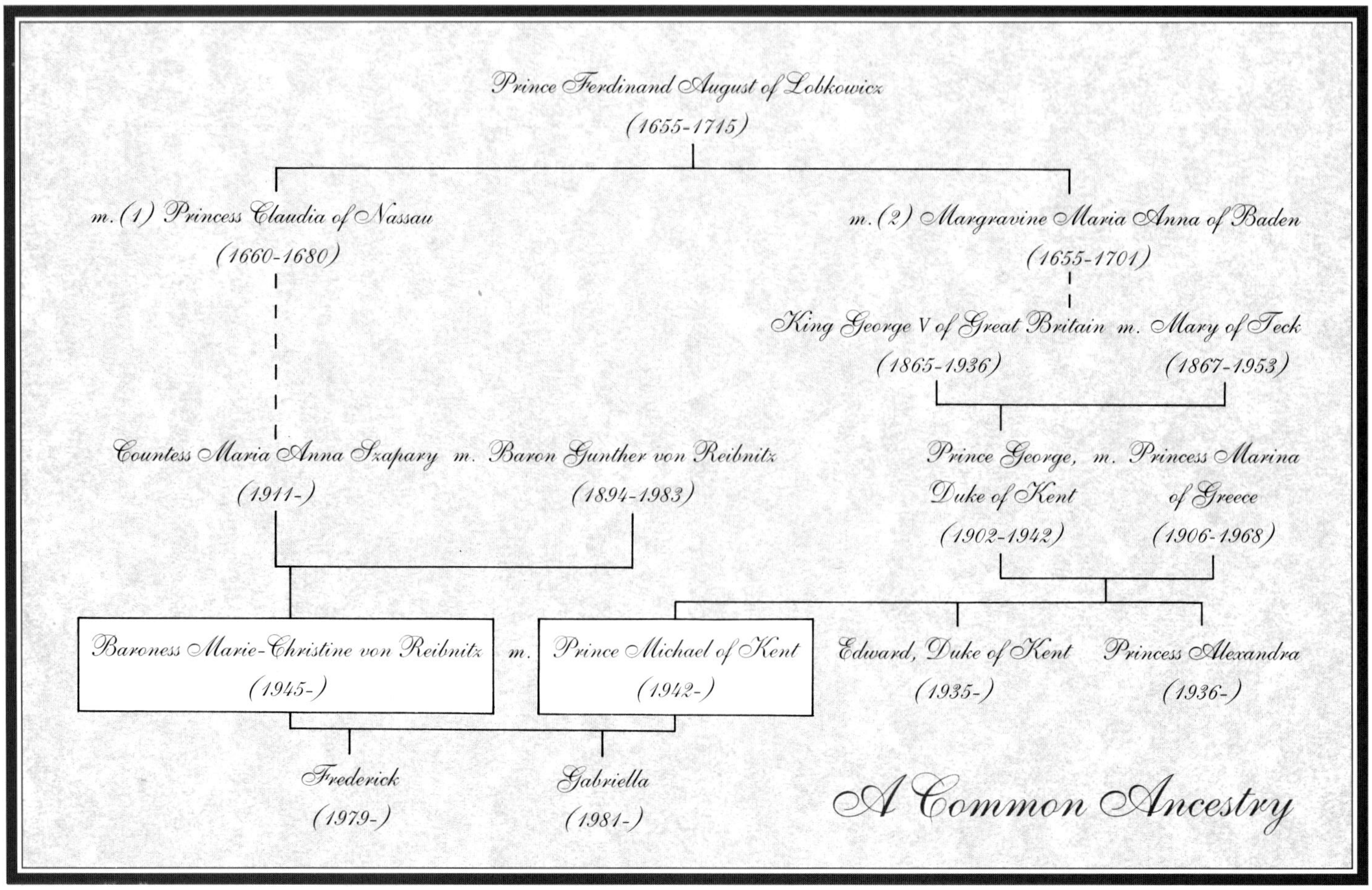
Prince Ferdinand August of Lobkowicz
(1655-1715)
m. (1) Princess Claudia of Nassau
(1660-1680)
m. (2) Margravine Maria Anna of Baden
(1655-1701)
King George V of Great Britain m. Mary of Teck
(1865-1936)
(1867-1953)
Countess Maria Anna Szapary m. Baron Gunther von Reibnitz
(1911-)
(1894-1983)
Prince George, m. Princess Marina
Duke of Kent
of Greece
(1902-1942)
(1906-1968)
Baroness Marie-Christine von Reibnitz
(1945-)
m.
Prince Michael of Kent
(1942-)
Edward, Duke of Kent
(1935-)
Princess Alexandra
(1936-)
Frederick
(1979-)
Gabriella
(1981-)
A Common Ancestry

and I were courting, I saw the family, and I had a jolly good look and I thought long and hard.'

But the view from the outside looking in is very different from the experience of being in the Royal Family, and watched by all. 'I would have been much happier and I think I would have had a much easier transition into the family if I had had a mother-in-law to help me,' Marie-Christine was to say later. Princess Marina, of course, had died ten years before the engagement and well before Prince Michael had ever met his bride-to-be.

The lack of a mother-in-law continued to bother Marie-Christine for a long time to come. 'The Duchess of Gloucester, for example, had the benefit of her mother-in-law, an older, benign guiding hand, as did my sister-in-law, the Duchess of Kent. I think that if I had a mother-in-law I would not have made some of the mistakes. I have had it said to me, "Why didn't you ask for help?" but who do you ask?'

But the waves Marie-Christine caused in the run-up to her marriage were mere ripples compared with what was to come. She knew that she was different – 'I was unsuitable, quite unsuitable, as a Royal bride. I am Catholic and I

⚜ *The newlyweds emerge into the Austrian sunshine after their wedding in a Viennese registry office below. As Marie-Christine was divorced, they could not wed in an Anglican church; and to ensure their children's place in the line of succession, they could not wed in a Catholic church either. However, as Royals, nor could they be wed in a civil ceremony in Britain. The only solution was a registry abroad*

'*We didn't realize we would be so public. We thought we'd be able to slip in under the woodwork*'

MARIE-CHRISTINE

Hulton Picture Company

William Wissing: *King William III* (detail) / Holburne Museum, Bath Bridgeman Art Library

WED IN A FAR COUNTRY

Prince Michael and Marie-Christine's marriage plans were upset by the many difficulties presented by ancient English laws and conditions of the Church. The first problems were caused by the Act of Succession of 1701 passed during the reign of William III *left*. According to this act, Royal Family members in line of succession are not allowed to marry a Roman Catholic. So in order to obtain permission to marry Marie-Christine, Prince Michael had to relinquish his rights to the throne. In addition, the couple had to agree to bring up their children as Anglicans before the Queen, who must approve all Royal marriages, gave her consent.

However, Royal consent did not end the couple's problems. Another ancient law, which specifies that members of the Royal Family cannot be married in a registry office, again complicated matters. Because Prince Michael and Marie-Christine planned to raise their children as Anglicans, the Catholic church refused to marry them. The Anglican Church also refused because Marie-Christine was a divorcee, and the couple were forced to wed in another country

was also the first tall woman to marry into the Royal Family' – but she wasn't quite aware of how foreign her differences would appear.

A Royal misfit

The Royal Family are cultured, but the depth and degree of Marie-Christine's feelings and thoughts about art history, opera, theatre, and interior design contrasts strongly with their more matter-of-fact approach to these subjects. If she encountered some coldness within the family at the time of the engagement, she probably put it down to British reserve which would melt in time. Her champion, Mountbatten, after all, thought she was marvellous and she had no reason to believe that the rest of the family would not come round in time.

Nowhere to marry

Meanwhile the issue of the wedding itself was becoming a problem. Where was it to be held? Marie-Christine and Prince Michael both favoured the idea of a church wedding in England, but they immediately came up against a series of brick walls. Their first choice, a ceremony in an Anglican church, was ruled out because divorcees were not allowed to be married in church. The Catholic annullment was not recognized by the Anglican church.

'She sounds far too grand for us'

THE QUEEN ON
MARIE-CHRISTINE

♔ *The family welcomes the newly created Her Royal Highness Princess Michael of Kent into its fold* right. *Prince Michael's elder brother, the Duke of Kent* far right *with his daughter, Lady Helen Windsor* left, *and his sister, Princess Alexandra, attended the wedding in Vienna*

Dmitri Kasterine/Camera Press

Dmitri Kasterine/Camera Press

👑 *Among the Royal guests at the wedding were Princess Anne and Lord Mountbatten* left. *Not so much a friend of the family, more a fairy godfather, it was Lord Mountbatten – who had taken a paternal interest in Prince Michael's upbringing – who was instrumental in guiding the lovers through the pitfalls of official sanctions and Royal protocol (he even suggested Marie-Christine change her religion). It was thanks to his intercession with the Queen that the couple could celebrate their union in the time-honoured manner* below

They also looked at the option of a wedding in a Catholic Church. For this Marie-Christine had to seek a dispensation to allow her to contract a 'mixed marriage'. Unfortunately Marie-Christine had already made public their intention to bring up any children as Anglicans so that they retained their place in the succession. This meant that seniors of the Catholic Church felt unable to grant permission for the mixed marriage.

It looked as if they would have to be married in a registry office – but even this was denied them: members of the Royal Family are not allowed to have a civil wedding.

A Church wedding denied

The only alternative they had was to be married abroad, and they settled on Vienna as the city. Marie-Christine continued to hope that the Catholic Church would change its mind and allow them to be married in church. What she wanted as the venue was the beautiful Catholic Church in Vienna, traditionally the aristocrats' church, with the famous Vienna Boys' Choir accompanying the ceremony. To that end they had already drawn up a long and illustrious guest list that bristled with Royalty from Marie-Christine's side of the family. Among the guests they hoped to invite were senior churchmen.

A civil ceremony was to take place in Vienna Town Hall first – a legal requirement in Austria, and many other countries.

But in the event the Catholic Church stood firm: a church wedding would not be allowed. The ceremony in the Town Hall was the only one to which they were entitled. Marie-

Dmitri Kasterine/Camera Press

⚜ *For the reception in an old Viennese palace, Marie-Christine wore a beautifully romantic lace gown – which she would have worn to the altar had ecclesiastical complications not denied her a church wedding. And, true to style, she won the day, or rather, evening: even the waiting, hard-bitten pressmen gave her an ovation as she stepped out regally with her Prince right*

Gustav Veith: *View of Vienna, 1873* (detail)/Historisches Museum der Stadt Wien/Archiv fur Kunst und Geschichte, Berlin

A POSH WEDDING VENUE

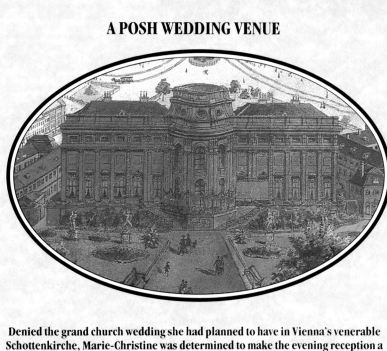

Denied the grand church wedding she had planned to have in Vienna's venerable Schottenkirche, Marie-Christine was determined to make the evening reception a memorable occasion. For this she chose the Schwarzenberg Palace, one of the old palaces of Vienna that had been the residences of the once-powerful Austro-Hungarian aristocracy and home to bygone splendours. The Palace had formerly been renowned for its gardens (now, sadly, not accessible to the general public). It was badly damaged in World War 2 but now, restored to its former glory, it boasts sumptuous rooms, such as the Marble Gallery where white stucco and gilded ornamentation offset the rainbow hues of the floor and walls

⚜ *Reliving the glories of old Vienna, Princess Michael glides to the strains of Franz Lehár's stately* Gold and Silver *waltz in the sumptuous, chandeliered setting of the Schwarzenberg Palace, taking her partner in life along with her far right*

Christine's grand plans had to be shelved.

The wedding took place on 30 June 1978 in front of 20 close relatives. Representing the British Royal Family were Prince Michael's brother, the Duke of Kent, with his 14-year-old daughter Lady Helen Windsor, his sister Princess Alexandra and her husband Angus Ogilvy. Princess Anne was the most senior member of the Royal Family to attend, and she was accompanied, of course, by her great-uncle and matchmaker Lord Mountbatten.

Marie-Christine wore a cream Hardie Amies suit – and for someone who favours romantic, flowing dresses when she can wear them it must have been a blow to be denied one at her own wedding. Prince Michael wore a plain, dark, double-breasted suit – he would probably have worn ceremonial regimental dress had he married in church.

Religious controversy

On the day of the wedding, Prince Charles was speaking at the opening of the Salvation Army's International Congress at Wembley. During his speech he made the forceful point that Christians were still arguing about doctrinal matters 'which can bring needless distress to a number of people'. It was assumed that this was a reference to Prince Michael and his bride being refused permission to marry in church. For his pains, Charles was soundly ticked off by the Catholic Archbishop of Glasgow.

After the wedding ceremony the day was given a romantic gloss by a spectacular dinner at the Schwarzenberg Palace, a 'particularly happy and brilliant evening', as everyone agreed afterwards.

After dinner there was dancing. The newlyweds, as tradition would have it, took to the floor first and by themselves.

In step together

'Michael and I opened the ball with the *Gold and Silver* waltz by Lehár,' Marie-Christine reminisced afterwards. 'My husband said, "Waltz?" and I said, "Waltz!" He murmured, "One, two, three, one, two, three . . ." And I said, "No, darling. Spin at quarter time." And that was the last time I ever said, "Follow me, I shall lead." He never quite got over the dizzying speed of the waltz but it started our adventure in life together.'

In fact, it did set the tone of their married life. Prince Michael was and is dazzled by his wife, who is too forceful a personality not to take the lead, especially with a husband who, while strong, is shy and retiring.

As Prince Michael has said, 'I believe that every man has a special place in his heart for one woman above all others.' This sentiment was symbolically expressed on the menu for that grand dinner, which was headed with the intertwined initials M and MC.

A grand celebration

In the middle of the evening the newlyweds led their guests outside into the park surrounding Prince Schwarzenberg's Palace. There they watched a magnificent staging of a performance by the Royal Opera Ballet Company, picked out by floodlights. After the performance was over they went back inside to continue the ball. At midnight the lights were dimmed, and a huge trolley laden with sorbets and sweets was wheeled in.

The newlyweds spent their wedding night apart. The Princess was hoping to be allowed to take holy communion on the following day, Saturday, but she was denied even this. Princess Michael was only allowed to attend the Saturday mass. She wore her cream wedding suit again, and went to church accompanied by a few relatives and friends. The final blow was that the main church had been locked and mass was conducted in a small room off an inconspicuous side entrance.

Spurned by the Church

To those who knew her it was obvious that Princess Michael was visibly upset by the public slight she has received from the Church she loved. That did not stop her from being an impeccable hostess to the guests for whom lunch was given at the British Embassy. Mountbatten, though, was moved by her sadness. He invited her to walk with him round the Embassy gardens, and while they strolled he urged her to think about changing her religion. His argument was that her church had treated her badly and that she owed it nothing. It would clearly have been a sensible and practical move, which would have removed problems for the Princess. But Mountbatten underestimated the extent of her religious conviction – a conviction that was to cause much heartache for herself and her husband in the years to come.

After lunch the honeymoon started. The guests gathered at the doors of the Embassy to see them off. The honeymoon destinations were pure Marie-Christine: Iran and India followed by another short stay in Vienna before returning to real life with Marie-Christine as the newest member of the Royal Family.

Dmitri Kasterine/Camera Press

♛ The elegantly proportioned manor house *left* is faced in the grey stone so popular in the Cotswolds. The sash windows and Jacobean-style chimneys show a striking symmetry which is reflected even in the shrub-lined approach

♛ This aerial view of Nether Lypiatt *above* shows the house set amidst 35 acres of lush grounds. The geometrically shaped flower beds at front and back echo the symmetrical theme, while the walled vegetable garden seen in the photo has since been replaced by a rose maze, containing 6000 roses, designed by the Princess

♛ The inviting open-air swimming pool *right*, in a delightful walled garden setting, is paved all around. Plants in tubs provide touches of further greenery

Tim Graham

NETHER LYPIATT MANOR

Prince and Princess Michael purchased Nether Lypiatt Manor, which is situated near Bisley in Gloucestershire, for £300,000 in 1981. The listed Grade 1 residence, built between 1702 and 1705, has been called 'the loveliest small house in Britain'. It has twelve bedrooms and five bathrooms, but measures only 46 feet square

THE LOVING COUPLE

ALTHOUGH PRINCESS MICHAEL WAS DISTRESSED THAT HER MARRIAGE WAS NOT RECOGNIZED BY HER CHURCH, THE COUPLE HAPPILY MOVED INTO THEIR NEW HOME, READY TO START A FAMILY AND SETTLE INTO MARRIED LIFE

T HE WEDDING IS A PEAK EXPERIENCE for any couple and it should have been perfect for the Prince and his new Princess. But the Catholic issue was not something that could ever be forgotten by someone as religious as Princess Michael. The problem was that she believed that in the eyes of the Church she was 'living in sin' with Prince Michael and she was anguished because she was barred from receiving Holy Communion. From the time she returned to London she began her campaign to have their marriage recognized by the Catholic Church.

But although this continued to occupy Princess Michael privately, she was too strong-willed and extrovert to let it dampen her spirits to any degree. She was now married to the man she loved, had become a Princess, and was for the moment the darling of the press. In the absence of the mother-in-law she wished she had as an adviser, she had decided to base herself on her own grandmother, Princess Windisch-Graetz, 'my model in all things. A very beautiful and grand Princess.'

Unheeded advice

Mountbatten was a constant visitor at their house. He was delighted with the new Royal he had sponsored and enjoyed her company enormously. At one dinner party he was reported to have said to her, 'Madam, the best thing you can do is keep your mouth shut.' As a fan of hers it is unlikely that he meant it as a reprimand, but he was probably serious. It was already becoming plain that Princess Michael scarcely knew the meaning of keeping her mouth shut.

Had Mountbatten lived he might have been the person to guide her through the pitfalls and into the heart of the Royal Family. As it was, he was killed by terrorists little more than a year after the Prince and Princess were married. The Royal couple lost a valued friend, for Prince Michael was hardly more knowledgeable about the ins and outs of British Royal protocol than Princess Michael herself. 'My husband hadn't a household of his own before our marriage, because he wasn't always around,' Marie-Christine was reported as saying.

Princess Michael, therefore, was left pretty much alone to build a structure to her new life. She knew already that there would be no money forthcoming from the Civil List, and in theory she could have opted out of public life, as Prince Michael already had. In practice, however, Princess Michael was very keen to

👑 **Below** *Newlywed, but not married in the eyes of her Church. The romantically lit, soft-focus photograph cannot hide the strain in Marie-Christine's eyes as she embarks on her five-year-long struggle to have her marriage recognized*

Norman Parkinson/Camera Press

become a 'real', high-profile Princess and to take her part in the duties associated with her new status.

Prince Michael was not as destitute as certain rumours would have it. It had always been known in the family that he would not be in receipt of Civil List money, so his family had made various provisions for him. His father had left him more money than the other children. It was put into a trust fund which was well in-

vested on the Duke of Kent's death and it had grown quite large by the time Prince Michael was allowed to touch it. Queen Mary had also left him a sizeable sum in her will, as had his other grandparents, Prince and Princess Nicholas of Greece. His mother, Princess Marina, had similarly left him a larger portion of her, admittedly, small estate than the other two children. All in all there was enough money to keep the Prince and Princess in fairly good style.

♛ *Prince Michael has always been a strong support for Marie-Christine. Perceived as something of an outsider in the Royal Family and subjected to a hostile press, she has relied on his staunch and unfailing love and support to see her through* below

Hulton Picture Company

♛ *As he is not on the Civil List, Prince Michael above has few regular Royal duties. This leaves him time to indulge his own interests, such as taking part in the London to Brighton Veteran Car Rally*

be a mother at last: she had longed for a child ever since she had married her first husband.

Lord Frederick Michael George David Louis Windsor was christened in the presence of the Queen and other members of the Royal Family. The Princess was besotted by her baby. 'I want to spend as much time with my children as possible,' she said.

But this exciting feeling came only with the first flush of maternity. Soon Princess Michael was to find the realities of motherhood too tough, messy, thankless and ordinary. She admitted regretfully that she was 'not a natural mother. I am no good at the practical side, which I leave to my first-class nanny.'

Distraught parents
It soon became evident that it was more than the practical side that she left to the nanny. And because of this, she developed very little idea of how Frederick and other babies 'worked'.

Frederick was only a few months old when Mountbatten was killed. The Prince and Prin-

'I always wanted to do everything I did as well as I possibly could'

MARIE-CHRISTINE

cess were appalled and desperately upset. With Mountbatten went Marie-Christine's most stalwart supporter and greatest friend in the Royal Family, and the nearest thing Prince Michael ever had to a father figure. That they were very close is supported by the fact that the Prince and Princess took over Mountbatten's work for the Variety Clubs International, a group that helps disabled children, and John Barrett, Earl Mountbatten's former secretary, came to take charge of their household.

By November 1980 Princess Michael was well into her second pregnancy. The thought uppermost in her mind was still the question of legitimacy, both of her children and her marriage, in the eyes of the Church. 'Have you any news about "Our Great Hope"?' she wrote to a friend shortly after the new Pope had been appointed. 'Now the second baby is on the way and the years drag on ... Let's hope this Pope finds a way to let us marry in Church at last.'

Lady Gabriella
Their daughter was born on 23 April 1981. She was christened Lady Gabriella Marina Alexandra Ophelia Windsor in the chapel of St James's Palace. This time the Queen Mother was pre-

Reports are mixed as to whether Princess Michael minded being left out of the Civil List. She is probably too practical a person to mind something which she could hardly take personally. Indeed, she has been known to say, 'We don't want to be on the list,' and even, tartly, 'I know how to work.'

Lord Frederick
Almost exactly nine months after their marriage, the Princess gave birth to their first child, a son, on 6 April 1979. Princess Michael's first proud reaction was, 'Look at his lovely big hands! He should make an excellent plumber.'

The baby was born at St Mary's Hospital, Paddington. He was delivered by the Queen's own surgeon-gynaecologist, Mr George Pinker.

The Princess stayed in hospital for five days before taking the baby home to their apartments in Kensington Palace. She was thrilled to

sent. The Princess was thrilled to have 'one of each' and she and her husband decided that their family was now complete.

Prince Michael's life had changed radically on marriage. In 1978 he was advised that he had gone as far as he possibly could in the Army hierarchy. Because of his Royal status it was unlikely that he would ever be posted to Ulster, which was an essential move in the career of an Army officer. It was hard for him to make the decision to leave, but Marie-Christine encouraged him, and in 1980 he resigned, with the express purpose of making a career in industry and commerce.

A new career

Then there followed a short nail-biting period when he had no work to go to. As Princess Michael pointed out, 'We were trying to earn our living respectably by my husband getting work. But he couldn't advertise "PRINCE – AVAILABLE FOR DIRECTORSHIPS". He couldn't be head-hunted.' There was only one

Snowdon Camera Press

Richard Slade Camera Press

way to go about it, the bold word-of-mouth approach, and Princess Michael was exactly the right person to do this.

This paid off quickly. In 1981 he was offered a directorship with Standard Telephones and Cables, the British branch of the American multinational STC, and in 1982 became a director of Aitken Hume Bank. These posts brought in much more than the Prince's £11,000 army pay, and the money was important to both of them. A common phenom-

enon, shared by others who have suffered deprivations in childhood, is the feeling that it is 'never enough', that it could all evaporate. That was so in the case of the Prince and Princess, both of whom were brought up with the knowledge that a sudden stroke of fate – out of anyone's control – had changed their fortunes completely when they were very young.

For this reason, too, Princess Michael never gave up work entirely herself, although that had been her dream. She keeps her interior design company going even now, though these days she only feels able to act as a consultant. She too has some other business involvements in Britain and also in the US. In the later years of her marriage she took to writing in order to make some extra money.

More money coming in meant that the Prince and Princess did not have to dip into Prince Michael's inherited fortune, and Princess Michael was able to indulge her extravagant tastes in their family homes.

♛ **Above** *The proud mother with her first child. Marie-Christine hopes that her children will turn out to be like their cousins, the Ogilvys. 'They are the nicest children I know,' she has said*

♛ **Left** *Pregnant with their second child, Marie-Christine joins Michael as a spectator at the Badminton Horse Trials. An exchange of tender glances reveals the strength of the love which brought them together and cemented their marriage*

THE PRINCESS AND THE CATS

Princess Michael is famous for her cats, and they are notorious – virtually wild, spoiled Siamese and Burmese pedigree animals and a few moggies, hated by the residents of Kensington Palace. In fact, the Princess loves most animals: 'anything on four legs with fur more or less qualifies,' she has said – one of the few traits she shares with the people of her adopted country. Love amounts to passion when it comes to her cats, and her distress when one of them went missing touched a chord in the British heart: she received over 2000 letters of sympathy.

Prince Michael has learned to live more or less happily alongside the cats. After all, he did start off the collection by giving his wife a pure black Siamese as a wedding present. Princess Michael relates how he used to be driven mad by the cats dragging small animals they had caught to munch under the marital bed. 'Do we have to sleep on top of an abattoir?' he cried in despair.

When her children were young, Princess Michael would make up stories for them that centred around cats. 'I have a Griselda story I tell,' she said at the time. 'She is a witch I invented with a motorbike engine on her broomstick, and long black hair down to the floor with an orange stripe. She eats little fat children. Her efforts are usually foiled by the magic cat, a Siamese'

THE PALACE HOME

In 1979, shortly after they were married, the Queen offered them a home at Kensington Palace. Number 10 was the apartment that Princess Margaret had lived in at the beginning of her marriage. This ten-roomed, three-storeyed home is small by Kensington Palace standards – indeed, Princess Margaret had dubbed it the 'Doll's House'.

With Princess Michael's interior design training it was inevitable that she would make the place look beautiful, and – as she says of herself, 'I always wanted to do everything I did as well as I possibly could.'

She did not have to start from scratch. Prince Michael had inherited all the contents of Princess Marina's apartments at Kensington Palace on her death – and these included chimney-pieces and door furniture. She had lived on a much grander scale in apartments that were almost twice the size of theirs, so there were many interesting pieces for Princess Michael to choose from. Since Marina's death this treasure trove had been languishing in Hampton Court, dumped unceremoniously and uncatalogued in a remote attic waiting to be collected.

Soon Princess Michael was regularly dashing up to Hampton Court in her Range Rover and picking through the dusty collection to rescue the furniture that she wished to use. Some pieces went to Kensington Palace, others to their home in Gloucestershire, Nether Lypiatt. Unfortunately, before she had finished

going through everything there was a fire at Hampton Court which destroyed much of what was left. Even more unfortunately, the fact that the collection had never been catalogued meant that the full value could not be claimed from the insurance.

Many beautiful, exquisite and rare pieces

The proud parents pause outside St James's Chapel after Lord Frederick's christening below. The only disagreeable aspect of this happy day for Marie-Christine was that her baby son was still considered illegitimate by the Catholic Church

survived. The apartments of the Prince and Princess have many fascinating items: the silver Seals of England, belonging to Queen Mary, fine antique glass engraved with the letter N from Prince Nicholas of Greece, portraits of Princess Alice, Queen Mary, Prince Michael's father and other members of the Royal Family.

Personal touch

'There is not a lightswitch in the house that is not designed by me,' Princess Michael has boasted. 'Rooms are like people, they don't have to be grand or even in great good taste to be fascinating. People have charisma, rooms have atmosphere and that's what counts.'

The apartments look very different from when Princess Margaret inhabited them. The layout, of course, is the same: there are bedrooms and the nursery on the top floor (both children have their own rooms there) and there is another room for the nanny. There is also a kitchenette and small dining area on this floor, as well as two bathrooms. There is a small roof garden leading off the children's bedrooms. Princess Michael designed this and had it built before Lady Gabriella was born.

On the lower floors there are the Prince and Princess's bedroom with separate dressing rooms and bathrooms, a large study overlooking the courtyard and their private garden, a

Hulton Picture Company

formal drawing room, dining room, cloakrooms, kitchen, pantry and so on. The basement is the largest area, with offices for staff, such as ladies-in-waiting and security men.

The drawing-room is decorated with blue moire on the walls. The paintings are mainly antiques, but much of the furniture in this room is modern, including a low glass-topped table with an intricate arrangement of drawers to house some of their collection of priceless Fabergé eggs.

Most of the heirlooms throughout the apartments are from Prince Michael's side of the family, but in the bedroom Princess Michael keeps a few mementoes of her own. In a lighted archway she displays her small collection of delicate glass swans and photographs of her mother, father and other members of her family. On her dressing table is a bracelet and brooch that Prince Albert gave to Queen Victoria. This bedroom, cream-coloured from the wallpaper to the carpets, leads into an en-suite bathroom with a Victorian theme.

Opposite the bedroom is the study they share. Inevitably it is lined with the books Princess Michael has used to research her own book, and volumes that Prince Michael uses, including many original Russian texts.

Number 10 Kensington Palace very soon bore Princess Michael's stamp. It was instantly

👑 *Prince and Princess Michael of Kent ride in an open carriage during a Royal parade* above. *For two people who had been brought up knowing that they had 'come down' from a better way of life, their status in the Royal Family and their comfortable, sometimes grand, life style are factors that Michael and Marie-Christine do not take for granted*

👑 *Marie-Christine and two-year-old Frederick admire new-born baby Gabriella* left. *While the Princess loves her children, she admits to her lack of maternal instincts. She has never been 'an ardent nappy-changer' and has tended to leave the more thankless aspects of mothering to her nannies*

PA/Topham

obvious whose home it was, not just because the walls were lined with many pictures of the Princess herself. It was the sense of style that really marked it out.

Settling down

At the beginning of their marriage the Prince and Princess would rise at six to go riding with the Household Cavalry through Hyde Park. But Prince Michael became less keen on horsemanship after he had managed to ensnare Marie-Christine and make her his wife. In the early days too, Prince Michael was still in the army, working for the Ministry of Defence. It was his habit to ride to work on his 500cc Honda motorbike, wearing motorbike leathers. Princess Michael used to like to see him off, accompanying him to the door in her dressing-gown to kiss him before he left, and wave as he roared off towards Whitehall.

But, as in most marriages, life eventually settled down to a more normal and less romantic pattern. When he became a City man, Prince Michael developed the habit of rising at eight and eating breakfast by himself in the dining-room while reading *The Times* or opening his post. Princess Michael too began to develop a more leisurely start to her day, taking breakfast in bed while she read through her own mail.

The motorbike days over, Prince Michael's journey to work became more conventional, as befitted his Royal status and position as a director. A chauffeur-driven Jaguar was substituted to collect him and deposit him at work.

With Prince Michael gone, Marie-

👑 *Prince and Princess Michael share an affectionate moment on the merry-go-round at the Berkeley Square Ball above*

👑 *Princess Michael was determined to have her marriage recognized by the Catholic Church. Progress was slow, but she never let up totally, writing letters to senior figures in the Church or talking to them face to face when she could arrange it. The Prince and Princess eventually became acquainted with the most senior of Church figures, such as Pope John-Paul II below*

Christine's day really began. In the early days she would dress and then pop into the nursery briefly to see the children. But, as she frankly admitted, 'I rarely spend long stretches of time with the children during the day but see them often for short times.'

No two days were ever the same after the early morning routine, and this is still the case today. What Princess Michael does depends very much on her commitments to business or Royal duties. Some time each day has to be spent with her private secretary discussing her invitations, requests and other important items of Royal business.

Keeping fit has always had its place in the timetable. In the morning the Princess will either have an exercise class, or will find a partner for a tennis game. Shopping figures largely in her schedule, as does keeping up with friends, either by telephone or meeting to chat or have lunch. Sometimes Prince Michael is able to join his wife at lunch-time.

In the evening, when they are not entertaining, they regularly eat fast food in the kitchen with paper napkins, watching the news on television. Neither of them cares very much for wine, preferring to stick to water, either plain or mineral, or a drink such as vodka and tonic.

The Manor House

Weekends and some holidays are spent at their country house, the Manor House at Nether Lypiatt. This Grade I listed building was said by the locals to be haunted. Certainly, shortly after buying it, Princess Michael called in the local Catholic priest and Anglican canon – to bless the house, she says, though rumour has it that what took place was actually an exorcism.

It is in Gloucestershire that the Princess began to pursue more seriously her love for riding. In season she hunts whenever she can, and she has taken lessons in point-to-point rid-

ing, despite the fact that she is well over the recommended age. She insists that one of her ambitions is to be put on the cover of *Horse and Hounds* in her own right. But, she says self-deprecatingly, that she 'has too little talent and too many years'.

The life style of Prince and Princess Michael needs the support of a number of staff members, and has done from the early days. When they entertain – occasions that are usually spectacular affairs – they invite extra 'moonlighting' staff from Buckingham Palace to help out. All the staff are treated considerately, despite Princess Michael's reputation for a volatile temperament.

Quality time

As the children have grown older, Princess Michael still finds she spends little time with them, and occasionally she feels guilty. Prince Michael spends more time with them than she does; the Princess finds that days can go by in which she only sees the children for 20 minutes in all. This, though, she has described as 'quality time'. 'When I am with them, I focus, I zoom in on them,' she says. 'In those 20 minutes, I do believe we get an awful lot across to each other and they seem to me to be very happy, very easy children.'

Despite all, she enjoys her children and likes talking about them. 'Gabriella is already feminine and quite maternal,' she said when her daughter was a toddler. 'She seized her first doll with shrieks of delight.' As Gabriella has grown older her mother finds even more to admire. 'Very Kent but a bit more like me,' she has described her, and 'a cool intellectual really – but full of mischief'.

Perhaps she was even more proud of her son when he began to show signs of a first-class brain. 'Imagine, he reads *The Times* to us at breakfast!' she boasted when he was still very young. She sometimes likes to take the credit for her children's talent. When Frederick started boarding school she maintained, 'Oh, he'll be OK. He's got my brains, thank heavens, and not the Kents'.'

Her influence, when she chooses to use it, centres on the issue of behaviour. She says that she has taught her children to be 'that little bit more polite and take that little bit more trouble because I want them to understand quite early on that they have obligations. When they see their pictures in the paper, which they do sometimes, I say this is because you have a responsibility. You don't just get your picture in the paper because you're a good-looking child. You might see your picture in the paper because you belong to a family which has a great obligation to this country.'

But she was amused on one occasion when

Hulton Picture Company

she realized how little of the truth about their Royal status the children had grasped. 'They haven't yet realized completely that I am not like other mummies,' she said at the time. 'I was leaving for a fancy dress ball in a crinoline, tiara and with a Prince of Wales feather in my hair – frankly I felt like the sugar plum fairy. Ella said, "Mummy, you look just like a princess." "But mummy is a princess," I told her.'

Dispensation at last

The great turning point in Princess Michael's life came in 1983 when she finally won her battle for her marriage to be recognized by the Catholic Church. On 25 July 1983 the Pope sanctioned a dispensation allowing the couple to renew their marriage vows in a Roman Catholic Church. The ceremony, like a second wedding, includes blessing of the rings, prayers, readings from the Scriptures and a blessing of the union.

Princess Michael felt that her happiness was finally complete, that nothing really terrible could happen to her again. Little did she suspect the personal crises that were to follow in the years to come.

The Princess was overjoyed when dispensation from the Pope was finally granted on 25 July 1983. She wore the same cream suit to the validation service that she had worn to her wedding in Vienna five years earlier above. It was a simple ceremony held in Archbishop's House, Westminster, which included the blessing of the rings, prayers, readings from Scripture and a blessing for the couple. But although the event was kept very low key, the fact that dispensation had been granted at all was a subject of controversy among the Catholic community

Tim Graham

♛ *Above* Ella, Freddie and two furry friends
in the gardens at Nether Lypiatt, the family
country estate, November 1984

♛ Eight-year-old Ella and ten-year-old
Freddie swinging on a fence at Nether
Lypiatt *right*

The children of Michael and Marie-Christine

Stuart Newsham/Camera Press

Anthony Crickmay/Camera Press

♔ Surrounded by his toys, Lord Frederick Windsor *above* celebrates his first birthday in the nursery at Kensington Palace

♔ The winsome three-year-old Lady Gabriella smiles shyly for the camera *right*

Stanley Lenman/Camera Press

TREASURES OF THE HEART

The lives of Prince and Princess Michael of Kent have not always been happy but, like any other marriage where both partners are very much in love with each other, they share a fund of remembrances – of people they feel deeply about and places they are fond of. Their two children, of course, are precious to both of them, and photos recording those fleeting moments of childhood will always be held dear

Anthony Crickmay/Camera Press

♔ Lord Frederick and Lady Gabriella Windsor are their parents' pride and joy. 'I waited so long to have a baby that every moment I get with Freddie is a great joy,' Marie-Christine explained on the birth of her first child in 1979, while Michael delighted in bath-times – he would roll up his sleeves and splash along with the children. *Above* Five-year-old Freddie and three-year-old Ella – and their parents – romp on the slides

Richard Young/Camera Press

♔ Tanned and smiling in the West Indian sunshine, Michael and Marie-Christine pose for the cameras in January 1985 *left*. They had flown to Antigua to open millionaire financier and yachtsman Peter de Savary's St James's Club, and spent much of the month on the island. They later went on to Barbados

Dmitri Kasterine/Camera Press

Tim Graham

👑 Lord Mountbatten had been more or less a surrogate father to Michael and his brother Edward since the death of their father in 1942. He later became very fond of Marie-Christine, and she of him. Without his intervention, it is quite possible that the Queen would not have given the couple her permission to marry.

He is shown *above* taking a snapshot of a group of wedding guests in Vienna, June 1978: *from left to right* Count Törring, Princess Olga of Yugoslavia (Michael's aunt), Prince George of Hanover, Princess Anne, the bride and Princess George of Hanover

👑 *Left* Freddie leads Ella who is riding a Shetland pony, November 1984. The photograph was taken on the grounds of the family's beloved country estate, Nether Lypiatt

THE ROYAL OUTSIDERS

WHEN THE PRINCESS OF WALES BECAME THE PRESS'S NEW DARLING, PRINCESS MICHAEL BECAME THE WOMAN THEY LOVED TO HATE. NEVERTHELESS, HER SUPPORTIVE PRINCE HAS HELPED HER WEATHER THE STORMS SUCCESSFULLY

T HEY NEED A SOAP OPERA TO SELL newspapers and they've got a hell of a soap opera with the Royal Family,' Princess Michael once said wryly. 'They needed a bad girl and they've cast me in that role.'

But that wasn't always the case. When Princess Michael first swept on to the scene she was given the 'kind' treatment by the press. Here was a princess who looked like a princess, with beauty and style. They made much of her looks and her tragic background. She filled the gap, in a sense, until one of the more senior – but younger – Princes married.

When, in 1980, Diana first made her presence felt as the possible bride of Charles,

The press photographers line up behind Princess Michael left as she makes her way to a public engagement. Her striking looks and outgoing personality guarantee that she will never be ignored by the press – although they don't always treat her kindly

Princess Michael and the Princess of Wales are seen together below. Diana's appearance on the Royal scene marked the end of the period of Princess Michael's favour with the press; they now began to turn a more critical eye on their former darling

Princess Michael was no longer necessary to fill the fairy princess slot. As Diana went on to become Princess of Wales she exceeded everyone's hopes in this area. She too was beautiful, tall and stylish. But she was also young, shy, charming, pure and unsullied. Princess Michael was now in for the harsher spotlight of the critical press.

She was right that the press needed a bad girl. Decades ago it had been Princess Margaret who could do no right in their eyes. Later Princess Anne took her turn. But as the 1980s marched on, Margaret had taken on the mantle of the 'poor thing' and Anne was well on her way to becoming a modern heroine. It was perhaps inevitable that Princess Michael was to become the next Royal target – she was certainly visible enough.

Hostile press

'Princess pushy', as the press unkindly dubbed her, has never known how to keep a low profile. Even when the press has obviously been gunning for her she has not been able to keep quiet. Part of the problem is that she finds it hard to figure out what it is she does wrong. Usually she puts it down to jealousy. 'Because I have a handsome husband, two beautiful children, two beautiful houses and am a naturally happy person and because it appears I survive the blows directed at me, the blows get bigger and bigger,' she has said.

The fact is that she provides them with all the ammunition they need. As even she agrees, she will keep putting her foot in it. Before public appearances, she admits, 'I always say a little prayer, "Please don't let me make a gaffe."'

The prayer rarely works. There she is, all dressed up, smiling, doing and saying the right thing and giving a good impression, when she spoils it all by saying about her charity work 'I don't go about thinking I'm going to enjoy it,

Hulton Picture Company

Anwar Hussein

but "Let's do our very best to ensure everyone enjoys it, so they get their money's worth."' No one likes to feel patronized, and British Royalty are very good at appearing to enjoy their work. No wonder the press fasten delightedly on Princess Michael's gaffes. 'I don't like it,' she says again of her charity work 'confidentially' to a friend, who rushes off to share the information. 'It bores me rigid most of the time – but I don't want that impression to come across.'

The press have also made an issue about Princess Michael's attitude to money. Again she lays herself open to attack. 'We'll go anywhere for a free meal,' she says jokingly of herself and her husband, and there are plenty of stories in circulation about the Princess charging to attend functions because, she says openly, she is not paid out of the Civil List to do so.

Meanness and an obsession with money are not attractive qualities, especially in people who are very much richer than the average. Princess Michael is probably as generous as almost anyone in the Royal Family, who are mostly careful with their money, but she is frank and ready to talk about the issue. For it is true that, however much she and her husband are able to earn, their ostentatious life style is expensive. Occasionally they sell off an article of value to top up their funds: a painting by Boudin that they owned went for £15,000, and

☙ *Princess Michael attends an awards ceremony for the Horse Rangers Association at Hampton Court above. Although she has, in the past, expressed a general dislike for public engagements, the Princess takes a special interest in, and serves as Royal Patron for, a number of organizations – such as the Horse Rangers, the Breast Cancer Trust and the Society of Women Artists, among others. She takes her commitments seriously and is a very active and valued patron*

☙ *Prince Michael and his son, Lord Frederick, embark on their first flight in a hot air balloon together right. The Prince's children are rarely seen in public with their parents and, unlike some of the other Royal children, the press does not dog them. Because of this Frederick and Gabriella are left alone to grow up in a relatively normal family environment*

Tim Graham

PA Topham

Anwar Hussein

'They needed a bad girl and they've cast me in that role'

MARIE-CHRISTINE ON THE PRESS

♔ *While the Queen appears to get along well with Princess Michael* left, *there is a fundamental difference of interests and personalities that divides them*

♔ *One interest that Marie-Christine shares with the other Royals is a love of horses* below. *Efforts to develop her riding skills have been supported by more experienced Royal riders. But it is probably sheer determination, rather than experience, that sees her through difficult riding events.*

The problem is mainly that she's not their type, and they are not hers. If her relatives were not royal it is unlikely that she would want to invite them to her glittering dinner parties, which she peoples with guests who are brilliant, witty and famous in their own right. She and the other Royals have few interests in common, apart from horses.

Pulling rank

But the Royal Family also resent the 'grandeur' which the Queen first suspected was there when Lord Mountbatten told her about Princess Michael. The Royal Family don't believe in pulling rank; they don't feel they have to. But Princess Michael does so ostentatiously. 'I know how to be a Princess,' she says, 'to give people good value for money.' The implication, of course, is that other princesses don't do as good a job as she. She knows herself that she is 'ambitious in the way that English people do not seem to be'. But she is incapable of changing the way she acts, despite the fact that it often annoys the Royal Family.

Prince Charles is said not to like Princess Michael very much, and although they are neighbours in Kensington Palace they communicate through memos or via their staff.

they have been known to sell off some of their solid silver cutlery and candlesticks.

But despite her unpopular image Marie-Christine doesn't stay down. 'I'm never unhappy,' she says. 'I'm momentarily unhappy, but I never allow myself to remain unhappy or depressed. I just go out and do something about it.' She has a fighting spirit.

Friendship betrayed

There are relatively few times that she has remained upset over anything that has appeared in the press, and one of those was when her friend and neighbour, Jilly Cooper, wrote a piece about her. It wasn't very unkind, but Princess Michael felt that her friendship had been betrayed. Shortly after it appeared she retaliated by sending Jilly Cooper a bag containing 30 pieces of silver. Jilly was upset, but her husband, Leo, put it all on a racehorse — which came in first.

More disturbing to Marie-Christine is her lack of acceptance by the Royal Family. 'I come very, very low in the pecking order,' she says, but, although it is true that she and Prince Michael are relatively junior in the Royal hierarchy, it is not a question of rank. Princess Michael frankly does not fit in.

The press would have it that the other Royals refer to her as 'Our Val' — as in Valkyrie. In fact her nickname in the Royal Family is 'MC', shorter and less affectionate.

Anwar Hussein

🜲 *The Daily Mail story above is just one of many run in the spring of 1985 exposing the Nazi connections of Princess Michael's father, the Baron von Reibnitz. Prior to this, she was unaware of her father's Nazi past, so the stories came as a complete shock. However, she soon realized that these 'revelations' were only half-truths and, armed with the facts, she faced the press to put things right*

Diana likes her more than he does, but sometimes finds it hard to deal with Princess Michael's personality. When Marie-Christine first visited Highgrove, the Gloucestershire home of the Prince and Princess of Wales, she gushed, 'What a beautiful house! But what a pity you didn't ask me to help redecorate it.'

That time Diana chose to be amused, but she knows full well that Princess Michael has referred to her patronizingly as 'the Sloane Princess' and to her best friend, the Duchess of York, even more damningly as 'the Coronation Street Princess'.

Princess Michael has managed to get on the wrong side of the Queen as well. She once arrived at a dinner given by the Queen an hour late. 'Please don't get up, anyone!' she said breezily as she sat down. But the Queen has a sense of humour, and she is likely to have been more amused than shocked by that incident. Less amusing was the Princess's remark that 'I sometimes feel like shooting the Queen's corgis.' She has also blotted her copybook during the Royal Family Christmas by complaining about the room she was given on one occasion, and insisting on having her dinner brought up to her room at another time.

Royal enemies

That there is little love lost between Princess Michael and Princess Margaret is no secret. It

'*I know how to be a Princess*'

MARIE-CHRISTINE

is a shame that these two have never become friends, and the cause of their discord is a secret between them. Outwardly they would seem the most alike of all the British Princesses. Princess Margaret is the most likely to pull rank of any member of the Royal Family, and both of them have a theatrical personality and a liking for friends who are well known and well respected, giving dinner parties reminiscent of artistic 'salons'.

The first hint the public had of Princess Margaret's dislike of Princess Michael came, oddly, through her son. In November 1983 Lord Linley was asked by a magazine what present he would give to his worst enemy. He replied (in the full knowledge that it would be printed), 'dinner with Princess Michael'.

Princess Michael was understandably mortified and upset. She kept her dignity by saying to the press that she was sure that Linley had been misquoted. However, she waited in vain for an apology, and they haven't spoken since.

That Christmas Prince Michael challenged Linley to his face. 'What was the meaning of that remark? Explain yourself,' he demanded. When Linley failed to think of anything to say the Prince continued, 'I hope you realize that you are talking about the woman who is my wife, the woman I love and the woman that *you* don't know.'

For the truth is that Linley did barely know

THE PRINCESS AS WRITER

In 1985 Princess Michael's first book was published by Weidenfeld & Nicolson – an historical look at eight famous women who had become Queens in foreign lands. She turned to writing because, she said, 'I used to be a very successful interior designer, but once I married Prince Michael I couldn't continue. What was there left for a mad princess to do decently? History seemed a safe subject.'

The pre-book publicity was terrific, and Princess Michael's gift for providing a good quote came into its own. 'I am not sure that it is going to be great,' she said. 'Probably as a first effort it will have far too much spotlight on it and not be allowed to sink as most people's first books are allowed to do.'

She knew that she could not win. 'For me to be loved, I should write a terrible book and fail. The English love failure,' she said. She had written the book for one reason, which she admitted: 'Even if I get terrible reviews I hope I shall be able to /cry all the way to the bank!'

As the hype continued, Princess Michael enjoyed her new image as writer. 'I would like my biographer to describe me as a writer who happened to be a Princess, not as a Princess who happened to be a writer,' she said.

But although she had also said 'I expect my writing to be criticized,' the criticism, when it came, took her aback. It wasn't the quality of writing that was the problem – it was that she had unintentionally lifted large chunks from other people's work. She had used a word processor into which she had typed her research and sometimes she forgot to rewrite the material. However, the book, a successful first attempt, did reach the best-seller list

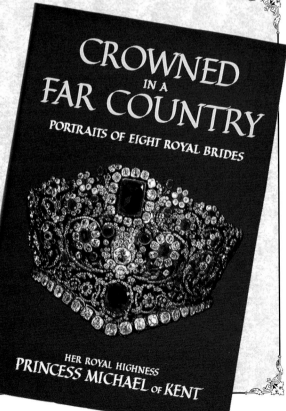

CROWNED IN A FAR COUNTRY

PORTRAITS OF EIGHT ROYAL BRIDES

HER ROYAL HIGHNESS
PRINCESS MICHAEL OF KENT

Hulton Picture Company

Princess Michael. (He was also once quoted as saying 'which one is he?' when Prince Michael's name came up.) His information came from his mother, whose anti-Princess Michael feelings were well known. Lord Dudley, a friend of Princess Margaret, wrote a satirical poem about Marie-Christine to be read out at one of Margaret's dinner parties in 1984. Although the guests found it funny, it was very cruel, and somehow it got into Prince Michael's hands. He was enraged, and showed it to a libel lawyer. On the basis of his advice, Prince Michael asked for and received a fulsome apology and a financial settlement for damages.

A devastating shock

The nature of her relationship with the other Royals subsided into merely a minor annoyance in April 1985, when a completely unexpected and devastating event occurred. Nearly seven years after her marriage, a newspaper turned up the fact that her father had once been a member of the Nazi party. 'Princess's father was in SS and Gestapo,' screamed the headline. It was a popular tabloid, and the full horror of it did not hit the Prince and Princess until they sat watching the six o'clock news that evening. 'Eighteen minutes were devoted to this story and showed old footage of Nazi atrocities,' Princess Michael recalled later. 'I was physically sick and the whole time my face was in cameo in the corner of the screen.'

The fact that her father had been a Nazi had been kept from Princess Michael, so initially she thought the story was make-believe. 'I immediately telephoned my mother ... and I said more or less ... "Guess what they are trying to pin on me now?" And she said, "But I'm afraid that it is true."'

Brought up only to know about her parents' stand against the Nazis, she found her mother's revelation almost unbelievable: 'It was a total shock to everything I have been taught to believe.'

👑 *Prince and Princess Michael are seen at the Badminton Horse Trials in April 1985 above. This was the Princess's first public appearance following the scandal linking her father to the SS and, though she was greeted by cheers from the crowd, she seemed serious, even tearful. However, this was not to be the only damaging press attention she would have to face this year*

Later the shock still had not sunk in. 'It is like suddenly discovering you are adopted. Here I am, 40 years old, and I discover something that is really quite unpleasant and I shall have to live with it.'

Princess Michael was determined to find out the truth for herself first-hand. She asked the Berlin Documents Centre to send her all the material relating to her father. It was true, of course, that he had been a Nazi, but her parents' version of how he had become disillusioned and spoken against the regime was also true. Princess Michael was relieved to discover that most of the journalists' 'revelations' were twisted half-truths.

Against the advice of Buckingham Palace, she insisted on giving a television interview about the subject shortly after she found out the facts. It was the right decision. She came across so well that when she turned up at the Badminton Horse Trials a few days later, she was cheered by the crowd.

Hurtful allegations

Later that year the newspapers ran another story about her alleged too-close friendship with Texas businessman John Ward Hunt. But although the allegations upset her and her husband, they weathered them and their marriage

Topham

👑 *The Amazing Greats Children's Party in London's Battersea Park is attended by Prince and Princess Michael above. The Royal couple make regular appearances at charity events and public functions, and occasionally undertake official engagements on behalf of the Queen, despite the fact that they receive no money from the Civil List to carry out these duties*

has continued to flourish.

The precise nature of their relationship is difficult for outsiders to know. Princess Michael is so much larger than life that her husband and her marriage are overshadowed by her vivacious personality. Some people say that she bosses him around and puts him down at her dinner parties, and they assume from this that the couple are no longer in love.

But this is too superficial an interpretation. Princess Michael says of her husband, 'people think I am the strong one, but he is my rock. He never fails me.' He is the quintessential strong, silent Englishman and he is quite content to let her take centre stage in all her extrovert foreignness. For, as she says, 'The whole key to me is foreignness. But because I talk English like an English person, have English colouring, lead a very English life, people subconsciously expect me to be English in every way. But I'm not – I'm as foreign as could be.' This is something that she often reiterates.

Another clue to their relationship is Princess Michael's stated belief that 'I think the purpose of my life is to improve the quality of my own life and those that touch me.'

A high-profile Princess

Princess Michael continues to be more high-profile than senior Royals such as the Duchess of Gloucester, but she must be relieved that press attention seems unaccompanied by spite these days. Whichever way the wind blows, she is prepared to weather it according to 'the philosophy of life I was brought up with. Good things happen and bad things happen, there are good people and bad people and you must keep your head above water and go on the way you were brought up, believing in and doing what you know to be right even if everything goes against you.'

Her charity work might not be of consuming interest to her, but she does it conscientiously, choosing causes in which she can involve herself closely, including the British Ski Federation, Breast Cancer Research Trust, Society of Women Artists, Royal Shakespeare Theatre Trust, Ponies of Britain, Arab Horse Society and the Royal Society for the Prevention of Accidents Tufty Club.

But the idea of Princess Michael slipping into a quiet and worthy middle age is unthinkable. It is likely that Princess Michael's sheer flamboyance, enthusiasm and hot-headed independence will land her in some kind of trouble again in the future.

Best friends

The person who sees her through times of trouble is, of course, Prince Michael. They are very close and she acknowledges that they have had a catalytic effect on each other. 'When a man marries he changes, he has responsibilities and when he has children he changes again,' she says. She knows that he is different from the man he was before they married, but she doesn't take personal credit for it. 'It was all in him just waiting to come out. It wasn't me. I just turned the key, he opened the door and came out into the light.'

On the other hand, she feels indebted to him for the part he has played in her life. 'He has

♛ Prince and Princess Michael, their children and Sponge, the family labrador, gather on the steps of Nether Lypiatt for a formal portrait below. This idyllic image dispels memories of the difficulties that both Michael and Marie-Christine have endured in the past – from their fractured childhoods up to the more recent press speculations that have tested their relationship. But despite the strains, neither has ever asked for special treatment or sympathy. Instead, they cope with their problems together, and together they'll be able to face whatever surprises the future holds

done an enormous amount for me. He has tried to teach me tolerance and patience and has taught me to take a deep breath and think before I speak – not that I always do. He is such a wise and underestimated man.'

His obvious continuing adoration of her also helped her through the difficult transition of turning 40. 'I had really dreaded reaching 40. It seemed a terrible admission of middle age . . . which meant over the hill, which meant the autumn of life,' she said. 'But I didn't accept it . . . I realized that a woman doesn't really come into her own . . . until a maturity sets in.'

Maturity does seem to have set in, for both Prince and Princess Michael. And it is this maturity, combined with the deep and supportive love they have for each other, that will see them through whatever the future has in store.

'*He is my rock. He never fails me*'

MARIE-CHRISTINE ON MICHAEL

Anthony Crickmay, Camera Press